Read what others are saying about this book:

"I was blessed by Borrowed Joy's moving, compelling testimony and as a **journalism graduate, newsman,** and free lance **writer,** I believe your story has tremendous journalism merit." Jim Daily, Director of **Public Relations,** In Touch Ministries

"Story of *Borrowed Joy* is deeply moving and well composed. I compliment you not only on the excellence of writing but the strength of character evident in your putting these experiences and thoughts on paper. Many will benefit from your sharing these and the obvious growth you have accomplished since the losses in your life. Coleen Grissom, **Dean** of Students, Trinity University

"That *Borrowed Joy* is a true story becomes quickly evident from the power of emotions that flows throughout the story. Confusion and emotional strain are easy to accept and empathy is immediate. Beautiful because of the courage it imparts, the story is direct and purposeful from beginning to end. As a statement it is concise, clear, and agonizingly direct." Sal Torres, **Student**

"Thank you for sending *Borrowed Joy* . . . I encourage you to continue and publish. It is solid, honest, sincere, and not the least bit hokey." C. Everett Koop, M.D. **Surgeon** General (Retired)

"Thank you for sharing *Borrowed Joy*. I hope you publish it. In tears as we read, we were encouraged by the theme, God is bigger than any experience." Larry Amundson, Athletes in Action, **Sports** International Project Director

"Thank you for *Borrowed Joy*. Words cannot express how we hurt for you. As no one else, you can understand when another shares similar circumstances. You have encouraged us. Claudette Reiser, **Counselor**, *Focus on the Family*.

"*Borrowed Joy* impacted the lives of many people here and brought encouragement to our lives. I encourage you to share these writings with others. Doug Thompson, **Counselor**, Word of Grace.

"Thanks for sharing this beautifully written experience. Three of us have read it and all agree it is <u>special</u> and should be made available to those it will encourage and help." Suzanne Moore, **Friend**, Mini-Mansions **Book Store**

BORROWED JOY
VICTORY OVER TRAGEDY

Bill, Dianne, and Steve

(David's pictures were burned.)

BORROWED
JOY

Victory over Tragedy

ABBA PUBLISHING
San Antonio, Texas/1991

Borrowed Joy -
Victory over Tragedy
By Della Pylant
Published by: **ABBA Publishing**
Post Office Box 47910
San Antonio, TX 78265–7910

Copyright © 1985
First Printing A 1991
Printed and Bound-United States of America
LIBRARY OF CONGRESS-
CATALOGING IN PUBLICATION DATA
Pylant, Della M.
Borrowed Joy-Victory over Tragedy
ISBN-9628285-5-6
Borrowed Joy-Victory over Tragedy
(Exerpt-Short Version) ISBN-9628285-4-8
Precious Gifts in Time of Grief
        (Exerpt) ISBN-0-9628285-2-1
Reaching out to Teenagers and Children
        (Exerpt) ISBN-0-9628285-1-3
by Della Pylant.–1st. ed.
Bibliography: p.
1. Grief–Sorrow (Victory over).
2. Death -(Recovery for parents)
      -(Recovery for siblings)
3. Reaching out to Others
4. Reaching out to children
5. Providing practical help in time of grief
LIBRARY OF CONGRESS NUMBER 90-083324
ISBN 0-9628285-5-6 $9.95 Soft cover
ISBN 0-9628285-3-X $14.95 Hardcover

To Hurting People Everywhere

Borrowed Joy is dedicated to you in the hope that you will come to know the touch of loving arms comforting you, of listening ears sharing your pain, and of tender hearts grieving with you until you find the true Peace in the storm.

Written for you who are in pain, Borrowed Joy ends in victory and recovery. You will be led through the pain and chaos, but also through experiences which slowly bring wisdom and understanding and finally release to face a brighter future.

Brief History of Author

Well-acquainted with tragedy and recovery, DELLA PYLANT (public school teacher, Alamo Writing Project fellow, college English and composition professor, writing consultant and speaker) reaches out to others through her speaking, writing, counseling, and listening.

TO BOOK AUTHOR AS SPEAKER, CALL: Leslie (512) 656-3269.

Foreword
by
Dr. James F. Jennings, M.D.

This story describes the emotional reaction to a tragedy far beyond that which most of us will ever encounter. Taken in its entirety, however, the story is about victory and healing.

My first meeting with Della Pylant came several years ago when she was speaker to a local class. A mutual friend had told me that through sharing her story with many others, Della vicariously leads them through the slow and painful process of recovery from the shock and debilitating agony following the loss of children. The listener feels her struggle with desperation and confusion, then is guided through incidents that bring fragments of perception to the writer before she finally arrives at the truth that leads from the "fearful chaos into wisdom and understanding."

Not only those who have lost a child or spouse and know the devastation of the post traumatic anguish, fears and nightmares, the stress, the doubts, the memories; but everyone who hears or reads the story seems to have experienced some event or circumstance which makes the story personally relevant.

Acknowledgements

I am deeply indebted to the following:

Dee Miller, Rene Baird, Mary Kott, Barbara Davis, Don and Leslie Pylant for critiques and support

Dr. C. Everett Koop, Dr. B. Thomas Haygood, and Dr. James F. Jennings for recognizing *Borrowed Joy* as a needed source for hurting people

Dr. Paul Gorsuch, surgeon, teacher and friend, for teaching me that faith in God is not just "pie in the sky someday" but comfort and guidance for all todays and tomorrows

Dr. Vernon Elmore for sharing our grief, speaking beautiful truths that pulled me back to reality, and bringing comfort and revelation

Brooke Army Medical Center staff for dedication to life saving then and now

Bill, Steve, and Don, my sons, for being my light ahead

Juanita, Illa, Patti, our families and friends who listened and cried with me, and allowed me time for grief

The fellow sufferers who shared their most intimate feelings and experiences during the recovery process

Cover Art by Curt Taylor

Preface

For the thousands of hurting people trampled by the random pain that sooner or later touches each of us, this bundle of pain wrapped in recovery is written with the touch of understanding that comes only from having experienced the pounding power of pain. Concise and agonizingly direct, it speaks of choices and effects of the only responses left to victims of each painful crisis, be they victims of abuse, violation, denial, loss, desertion, or disappointment.

Personal and intimate and necessarily giving part of the author's soul, the sensitive theme and powerful content of this book speak to the denial, shock, apprehension, resentment, anger, guilt, depression, and finally recovery and unique preparation. It speaks of power toward self-recovery in reaching out to others in similar situations. Addenda speak to the needs of grieving adults, teens and children and provide examples of fulfillment of those needs.

Contents

Borrowed Joy

"Oh, please, God!" I screamed. "You can't take her! She's ours! You gave her to us! Oh, please God! Don't take her! She can't die in that hideous fire by herself!"

The sirens echoed my agonized screams and pleas as the ambulance screeched away from the curb and rushed me toward the hospital.

A few hours earlier my husband and I had enjoyed our main Sunday meal together with beautiful, happy children who were our greatest joy. Bill was twelve years old; Steve, eight years old; Dianne, five years old; and baby David, eleven months old. We had moved into a new subdivision in the community and formed some close relationships with friends who possessed many of the same values we held: God, family, home, and friends.

Being family and friend oriented, we needed space for play and entertainment; hence, we were converting our carport into a den-playroom and adding practical furnishings. The room lacked a few finishing touches such as cranks on the casement windows. A twenty cubic foot freezer had been delivered and was sitting against the outside wall next to the front window and needed to be moved inside.

In the den that April Sunday afternoon, my husband watched television with the children for a few minutes. Then he said to Bill and Steve, "Come on boys, we need to go and cut Mamo's lawn and get back to take care of little David while your mother helps with your uncle's housewarming.

While they were gone, I finished in the kitchen, and Dianne stayed in the room with little David until he went to sleep in his crib. Then she went to pick some tiny, pink rosebuds from the vines climbing on the backyard fence. Using a rubber band and a paper doily, she made a nosegay, put it into a tiny pimento jar and placed it on my bedside table as she had done so many times in the past. She saved a few buds to give to me and to her daddy when he and her brothers came home. Since my husband had planned to cut our grass, he stopped at a filling station and picked up two gallons of gasoline for the power mower. Until the garage could be built, the only storage space was in the utility room.

My husband said to Bill and Steve, "Come on boys; David is awake and I need to take care of him so your mother can leave. We'll cut the grass when she gets back."

As I backed the car down the driveway, Dianne called, "Mommy, I forgot to give you your flower."

I waited for her to come down the driveway to the car. "Thank you, Darling, its fragrance will make me think of you while I'm gone. Now go inside," I said, as I hugged her again and then watched her go reluctantly into the house.

When I returned in the early evening, I found Dianne and David with their daddy in the den watching television and Bill and Steve in the back bedroom at the far end of the house playing with a toy train. Little David, hungry and sleepy, began to whimper. As I took him from his daddy, he cried out in pain. My corsage pin had stuck him. His daddy held him again so I could change my clothes. As I walked down the hallway, I heard a crash and went running back.

I met my husband bringing the baby to the bathroom.

"Wash the gas off David so he won't blister while I clean up the gasoline!" He hurriedly explained, "He threw the toy rabbit across the floor and crawled after it; he sat up and reached out, but instead of picking up the rabbit, he pulled over the gas jug and broke it."

I put the baby in the bathtub, but when I turned on the water, an explosion from the den terrified me.

Turning off the water and running back toward the den, I found my husband with the bottom of his trousers saturated with gasoline. His pants legs were on fire. He was starting out the back door to get the water hose.

"No!" I cried. "The wind is blowing; it will spread the fire on your clothes."

Picking up the entry rug just inside the back door, I smothered the fire on his clothing.

"The water heater caused an explosion!" he breathlessly explained.

"The house is on fire! What are we goin' to do? What are we goin' to do?" he cried.

"Don't panic; where's Dianne?"

"She's in the room with the fire!"

We ran to the den.

"Dianne, move as far away from the fire as you can; we will get you," I called to her.

The fire barred entrance to the area where she was. My husband turned over a chest and ran in to reach her. Fire billowed across the gasoline soaked carpet and encompassed that end of the room. The heat exploded the other gallon of gasoline. The only exit was through the front window.

"Take her to the front window. I'll take her from you there," I shouted as I ran around through the living room to the front.

The crank to open the window was missing. He threw his body against the window to open it. The window opened far enough for his body to lodge in it. The freezer was against it. His clothes were on fire. I could not move the heavy freezer to help free his body.

"Help! Help! Someone, help! Someone, help me! Our house is on fire! My husband, my little girl are in the fire! Someone, help! Oh, please, won't someone help me?" I screamed.

A neighbor on the next street jumped the fences and helped me move the freezer and dislodge my husband's body. The neighbor ran inside to see what he could do.

The metal casements sizzled my fingers as I tried to get in through the window to reach Dianne. My husband was lying on the ground with his clothes on fire. He was screaming in pain and begging me to help him. He was going to run.

"No! no! Roll, roll on the ground. Don't run! Roll! Roll!".

He was in too much agony to respond.

He just kept screaming, "Help me! Help me!"

I rolled him on the ground and beat out the fire with my hands.

Eight-year-old Steve had found his way out and tried several times to reach his sister. He had gone to a window on the opposite end of the house to tell Bill to come out through the window.

Red lights flashed circles of confusion. Sirens from ambulances and fire trucks shrieked their warnings. Neighbors and passers-by appeared from every direction. Everyone talked loudly and asked questions all at the same time. I pleaded, "Won't some of you hold on to Bill and Steve and keep them away from the fire?"

My husband broke loose twice from the people who were holding him, leaving his burned skin in their hands. Someone shouted, "Don't grab his arms; you can't hold him, and you're making the damage worse. Someone get a blanket." He managed to get back to the fire twice but couldn't find a way to get Dianne out. Finally, he was rolled in a blanket and taken away in an ambulance. I was taken across the street to a neighbor's house and laid on a couch.

As soon as I was laid down, I remembered David.

"I have to get David from the bathtub!" I cried out.

"David is out!" my neighbor assured me.

When our patrolman friend told me he would take the boys and the baby to my sister's house, I lost all grasp on reality.

As I lay on a hospital bed and medication began to wear away, hideous panic seized me and swept away my endurance. I knew I must not scream; yet I could feel my throat tighten, and I could hear the uncontrollable agonized moans slip past my lips, as my tortured brain was desperately and hopelessly trying to avoid the finality of the truth that our precious little girl had died alone in that shocking, horrifying, blazing fire. I could hear my mother through her tears trying to talk to me about a funeral.

"No! No!" I screamed.

"Della, you must help make plans for the funeral for Dianne and little David." she said.

"No, Mother! David is not dead!"

"Oh, my darling, the baby suffocated while you were trying to rescue Dianne."

A horrible moan escaped from my body. I screamed myself into deeper shock. I could not bear to have the bodies of my beautiful children put into the ground.

"No! No! No! Not my baby, too! O-o-oh God!" The shock was more than I could endure. I felt the sting of the needle containing medication that would drag me into obscurity.

Later, through a hazy semi-consciousness I became aware of a hand holding mine and a voice repeating words: "She wasn't alone; she wasn't alone."

Because I desperately longed to hear these words, they pulled me from my semi-conscious lethargy. I listened hard and tried to hold on.

"Della, she wasn't alone."

His hand engulfed mine and somehow

gave me something to grasp. At the same moment I heard this minister say:

"She wasn't alone! When we can no longer reach our children, God is there! In his strong, yet gentle arms, he lifts and comforts them."

More than anything in the world, I needed to know that my precious little girl had not been alone, but shock and apprehension mercilessly assaulted my brain with disbelief.

Numbness and emptiness ravaged and tore at the gaping chasm in my body. Fragmented thoughts and emotions tortured and paralyzed my brain. Drowning in confusion and pain, I screamed, "Why? Why? Why do I have to give them up? I can't! I can't! Am I never to feel Dianne's little arms around my neck again? Oh God, why?

Oh, this endless, grinding torture that returns and returns to questions with no answers! I need my babies. Oh, God! Only you know the answers! Oh, God! Why? Why would you take them after you gave them to us? Don't you care that we love them so much? Please help me!"

Again the pastor comforted: "Della, we don't know why this happened, but God does care. We think that if we can't help our children, no one can. But God is there. In his all-sufficient, gentle, yet strong arms, with the most tender love, he lifts and comforts them.

Even though we don't know what the world holds for us, we know they are safe from the sufferings of this world. Where God is, is the light that children love so much, the light that never goes out. They're together and they'll want for nothing. Our loving father knows so much better than we how to love and care for them. Della, your husband and your sons here need you very badly, and they are concerned about you."

This minister friend offered these words of comfort, and they sank deep within my troubled mind. He held my hand and prayed that God would fill the emptiness and give me the faith to reach out for the greater strength that he had promised in times of greater need. I, too, silently prayed to God. I felt his presence, and I knew he wouldn't leave me in the times ahead.

The following days were to prove this true when my strength and endurance were depleted many times. I learned to depend on God and each time saw the miracle of his strength made perfect in my weakness.

When the doctor visited me, he pointed out something I had not realized. "Della, your husband's burns are extensive. The burn ward at Brooke Army Medical Center has the facilities to give the care he needs, and they've agreed to take him since he is a veteran. I've sent him there where he can receive the best care available."

"However, according to his doctor, your husband is confused because he's heard different stories about the fate of you and your children. He is not cooperating in his treatment.

At times he seems to know your little girl died in the fire. Since he hasn't seen you, he thinks you may be dead and that he's not being told. If he could see you and you could tell him about the children, perhaps your being together would make it easier for both of you. His doctor believes that he would become a more cooperative patient."

I knew that I must go to my husband, and I knew that somehow I must attend the funeral of our children. I asked to be released from the hospital.

That night my brother took me to the funeral home. As we approached, beautiful and fragrant flowers overflowed the rooms into the hallways.

My body began to tremble uncontrollably as we approached the caskets that held the bodies of the children. I pleaded with them to open Dianne's casket, but my brother said they couldn't. Little David's body looked so beautiful and lifelike. I wanted so much to kiss him, but my brother held me back.

"Please, let me just kiss my baby on the forehead."

Finally, he walked closer with me. As I leaned forward and kissed that hard cold little forehead, the shock was horrible. My body crumpled in my brother's arms. As shocking as it was, that kiss brought home to me as nothing else could the finality of physical death. As beautiful as that little body was, that was not my baby. He and Dianne were at home with their heavenly Father.

With medication and the physical support of my brothers and relatives, I attended the funeral for our children. I remember having my head on my brother's shoulder, opening my eyes and seeing how beautiful little David looked, and longing to see the dainty body in the twin casket. I remember the minister speaking of no night and no darkness in heaven but always light and his repeating the word "together". "Together" began to ring in my heart.

As we left the chapel for the trip to the cemetery, my brain was tortured with jumbled thoughts and images that delicately balanced between reality and oblivion.

The cemetery was beautiful and peaceful as the minister spoke words of comfort and promise.

"Please! Allow me to stay behind for just a few moments," I requested.

Friends and family, not understanding my need to be alone, became concerned. I spoke to the minister.

"Please stay behind with me for just a moment. It's so hard to leave these little bodies to be lowered into the graves," I sobbed.

Kneeling beside the grave, I asked, "Will you help me pray?"

Tears rolled down his cheeks, and I saw him tremble. This had not been easy for him either, but once again he prayed for the cour-

age and strength that I needed. God did not fail
me.

The next day, my mother, a friend, and
the minister accompanied me to Brooke
Army Medical Center for my first visit. As I
walked into the cubicle, I searched for my
husband's face. A surge of panic washed over
me when I couldn't find him.

Then I heard him, "Oh, Thank God, I
thought you were dead; I wanted to die, too!"

Only the voice was recognizable; the body
was so swollen and dark. He began to sob
violently and to thank God that I was alive.

How could I tell him of the children's
death when he was so thankful that I was alive?

As we talked, he kept asking me, "What's
wrong? What's wrong?"

Groping for words and the way to say
them that would hurt him least, I felt weak and
uncertain. I looked out across the big parade

field in front of the hospital and silently prayed, "Oh, God, help me; I can't do this."

Then I knew the phenomenal strength that can become ours when we depend on God, and I found myself speaking to my husband.

"You must promise to listen to what I have to tell you and not interrupt until I have finished," I told him.

"What are you trying to tell me?" he asked apprehensively.

"Remember the tiny pink roses that bloom on our back fence and how perfectly beautiful they are as tiny buds, without a blemish and so much more intensely colored than the fully blossomed roses?"

"In his search for perfection, God found the most beautiful little bud at the height of its creation and sprouting beside it a tiny little bud. These two, he took with him to make heaven more beautiful and to guide our way."

"What are you saying?" he pleaded. "Oh,

no! No! Are you telling me that Dianne and David are dead? Oh, God, I tried to get her! Oh, I'm so sorry, so sorry!"

As we both sobbed, I tried to comfort my husband, "I know it's hard to understand why God would allow this. We had them just long enough to experience all of their wonder and love, just long enough to make us want them with us so much! Surely, time will dull this ache. Oh, how can memories bring so much pain?"

"But why?" he questioned. "Why? When we loved and wanted them so much, why are they gone? How will we stand it?"

He cried himself into the first sleep for many hours.

The road back to health for him was long and arduous. For months his suffering and delirium were like a hideous nightmare. He would become confused and apprehensive. Thinking he was on a roller coaster, he would plead for someone to stop it. Sometimes, excruciatingly he would scream Dianne's name over and over so loudly that I was afraid the screaming would cause his death.

The hours were indeed dark during the long time period required to get a good skin covering on his body, and so many people begged to help.

Letters and cards came from all over the United States, telling of peoples' prayers, reassuring us with their offers of money and services. Help poured not only from our family and those of our own faith and race, but also from many creeds and races.

A world of people put their resources at our disposal, and love abounded all around us, helping us through each new difficulty.

When friends who wanted to help with monetary gifts were told that we had a family financially able to help us, their reply was: "Please let us help in this way; it's the only way we can share this burden and express our love."

While my husband was in Brooke Army Medical Center, he was placed on a metabolic study with several young aviators who had been burned in a plane accident. The study proved very successful in combating dehydration and in helping the body accept the skin grafts. His life was spared under the conscientious care and skill of a kind and efficient staff.

His eventual physical recovery far surpassed what the doctors had expected and was classified as a medical phenomenon. Early in his treatment, the doctors said he might never walk again nor use his hands and arms fully. However, not only did he walk and use his hands and arms, but after several months he returned to his job. He performed his duties well, even with some of his fingers stiff and drawn.

When he went back to work, two friends came to be with me each day, bringing with them whatever work they had to do. Facing each day was still an effort and the taunting

"Why?" questions still tortured me. As I handled and treasured Dianne's belongings, each treasure painted memory pictures that brought a mixture of pain and joy.

One of my friends who came each day had a little girl just younger than Dianne. Patti always brought some of her favorite toys to play with. However, one day she looked up at me and asked, "Della, may I play with Dianne's dishes?"

I wasn't sure I could watch her play with the little dishes and not be overcome with emotion, but when I looked down at that little face, I couldn't refuse her. I brought out a small table and the dishes. When Patti began to play, it was as though Dianne were playing with them. I realized that I had been torturing myself by making idols of her things.

We kept a few treasures: the little brown felt hat with heart shaped ear warmers on the ribbon ties, the pair of sheer lavender gloves with white lace trim, some of her dolls, and her small red doll suitcase that always held her current treasures. Knowing that her clothes could bring comfort and her toys bring happiness to another child, we gave away the other things.

Even breathing was an effort. Inadvertently, I kept searching for resemblances to Dianne and David in other children. I had to discipline myself not to stare, but when I saw a child who resembled either of them, I wanted to take the child in my arms. Each time I heard a baby cry, my heart ached unbearably.

I continued to question, "Why?" When people told me they understood how I felt, I knew they believed they did, but that they couldn't truly know.

Then fragments of wisdom began to come from unexpected places and became a turning point for me. One day when I was having a difficult time and a friend was trying to comfort me, I looked up to see pain and tears in her eyes, and I thought to myself, "She really does understand."

Suddenly, for a moment, her tragedy became greater than mine. I remembered, "She has always wanted children but never been able to have them," and I thought, "Oh God, would I rather not have had them at all and never known all the wonder and joy they brought to our lives?"

For the first time I was able to say, not, "Why did you allow this to happen to us?" but, "Thank you God for giving them to us and allowing us to experience all of their warmth and love for a little while."

I said to my friend, "Please forgive me," and now I softly murmured, "Thank you, God, for enriching our lives with the sweetest part of theirs."

Volunteer work in a children's ward of a local hospital taught me many lessons in love. The cupcakes and the cookies, baked, decorated, and taken to the children for the holidays brought many hugs, smiles and unexpected rewards. I stayed with these children and gave the parents some time together for themselves. Each time I could do something for these children or their parents, I had the feeling that I was doing it for my own little ones. Nothing helped my healing as much as helping others.

Memories of past incidents have come back to me more than once and caused me to rethink many things. After we had two wonderful boys, God blessed us with a little girl who was sweeter and more beautiful than I had ever even dared to dream. Quick to smile, dainty, feminine, she loved little girl things such as ribbons, dolls, and perfume. Always ready for fun, she moved with a fawn-like grace as the ruffles on her dresses bounced in rhythm with her soft golden curls.

I recall her childlike faith when she awoke one night very frightened. Believing someone was trying to get into her room, with her heart beating very rapidly, she had come to our bedside. I hugged her and told her she could get into bed with us for a little while.

I went to check her room. Dianne followed me into the room and said, "Oh, Mommy, I forgot. See the ivy plant growing? That's God's way of showing he takes care of us, and the stars are little lights to show he is with us." She trustingly climbed back into her bed and went to sleep. God did say to come as little children, didn't he?

Dianne was very happy on her fifth birthday, at her party and afterward with her brothers. She modeled her new two piece sun suits and the dainty jewelry she had received as gifts. They were so proud of her, and as they went to play, Steve put his arm around her and told her, "Sister, when you go to school, you'll be the prettiest girl there."

A few days later she came in from playing alone in the backyard and told me, "Mommy, I saw an angel, and she told me I wouldn't be with you and Daddy and my brothers on my next birthday. She said I would have my next birthday in heaven with God."

I chided her about being truthful, but her

feelings were hurt that I'd doubted her. With quivering mouth and big tears she said, "But Mommie, I did see 'er and she did tell me ."

I picked her up and said, "Darling, sometimes it's hard to know what's real and what isn't, but I love you and I want you here with me."

Admittedly, many things I still do not understand. Nevertheless, I know that God is all-powerful, and I cannot deny his power to reveal himself to a child.

Although in this world less than a year, brown eyed and blonde little David, with a fun-loving personality quickly gained the adoration of his family. Rattling the sides of his playpen, he would let us know when he was ready for some play with his family.

Responsive to our attention, he would look us straight in the eye, and with the cutest expression, he would twist his little head and listen as though he understood exactly what we were saying. Then he would laugh from deep in his tummy the most satisfying chuckle until he had us all laughing at nothing. This little bundle of love left a great void and many unfulfilled dreams in our lives.

At strange times, comforts came. Months after the fire when my husband and I were talking together, I said, "I wonder why Dianne didn't cry out to us."

He told me, "Oh, I thought you knew! She must have suffocated because I had her in my arms and as I was telling her, 'Daddy has you and will get you out,' she was hugging me, and her body became limp. I laid her in the playpen to throw my body against the window."

"Oh, I didn't know! Thank God she wasn't alone!"

Truly, the dark times as well as the bright are necessary to weave the pattern of life, and when all is finished, we'll know the reasons for the dark times as well as the bright.

Tragedy never leaves us the same, but it

leaves a choice. We have the choice to either grow and learn a great lesson in compassion or to become bitter and cut off our sources of comfort and healing. Our choice touches the lives of those around us, most of all, those who love us.

More and more I am learning that when we trustingly reach out to him and follow his leadership, our God brings us from fearful chaos into peace and from darkness into light.

Afterword
Dr. James Jennings, M. D.

AFTERWORD
by
James F. Jennings, M.D.

The last paragraph of this story is classic as it recognizes God's sovereignty and his power not only to bring us though the most difficult times in life but also to use these experiences to bring strength, compassion, and usefulness.

Perhaps no greater stress attacks the emotions than the loss of a spouse or children. Eventual healing can take a long time and, tragically, never comes to some, not because it can't, but because God's total healing power is never appropriated.

Difficult though it may be to understand, the Bible teaches that Jesus, the author and finisher of our salvation, was made "perfect through sufferings" (Hebrews 2:10), and that he was "a man of sorrows and acquainted with grief." Because we have been created by Him and are made in His image, only He has the full knowledge, insight, and ability to give complete healing.

In his wisdom Christ allows all things into our lives to help conform us to His own image. When we can accept this and recognize that His perfect thoughts and ways are not always ours, we can view circumstances and events, not with a fatalistic attitude, but with insight from an eternal perspective.

When a catastrophe such as described in *Borrowed Joy* occurs, questions are often asked. "Why did the children have to die?" and, "What will happen to the children?"

As to the first question we can speculate why, but only God knows the answer. We know that "children are a heritage from God." He gives them to us for our own instruction, joy and maturity, and so that we may prepare them for His service. In His permissive will they are sometimes taken before we expect, and in this life God may never reveal His purpose.

Three scriptures are particularly helpful in answering the second question: Matthew 18:10, I Corinthians 7:14, and II Samuel 12:22-23. We find that children have a special place in God's eyes and are assigned a guardian angel and that children of believers are held in special recognition. On the death of his son, David said, "Can I bring him back again? I shall go to him, but he shall not return to me." We know that if our children die, we will see them in heaven.

Sometimes understanding why an event occurs takes years, and in some instances we may never fully understand in this life; however, we are asked to walk and "live by faith." When we do this, we find that in God's appointed time, we will understand. Until then, we can trust that ours is a daily process of being conformed into the image of Him, by whom

and for whom all things were created. Such is
the story of *Borrowed Joy*.

Help?
Let Me Count the Ways
by
Della Pylant

Help?
Let Me Count the Ways!

Loving, you brought comfort,
Overcoming, you conquered chaos,
Visiting, you said, "I care."
Embracing, you shared grief.

Helping, you revived strength,
Encouraging, you imparted belief,
Listening, you released pain,
Praying, you restored faith.

Encouragement, help, and strength, far beyond expectations poured from many people, helping us out of sudden disaster and chaos. To express the feelings of gratitude in our hearts, words fail completely. With the passage of time, we learn more and more of our inability to comprehend the many things done for us.

My husband and I lay in a hospital, he with the major part of his body in second and third degree burns, coupled with shock from the death of our two children. We had not yet begun to think of the material losses to our home and business and of our need for a support system to help us through this crisis, but many others had thought of it and were moving in numerous ways to help us.

A world of people seemed to put its resources at our disposal, and love abounded all around us, helping us through each new difficulty.

Family, friends, and acquaintances requested, "Please let us help in this way; it's the only way we can share this burden and express our love." They had deposited money into our bank account after paying for our children's funeral. Loving care, encouragement, and help poured not only from our family and those of our own faith and race, but also from those of many creeds and races.

Many more donors than needed replenished the local blood bank, thereby spreading the generosity of our families and friends to help others as well

Our civilian doctors along with two family members worked with army personnel to acquire access and move my husband to a military hospital known world-wide for its treatment of burns. Because he was a veteran, he received multi-thousand dollar treatment at this facility under the conscientious care and skill of a kind and efficient staff, and civilian doctors refused payment for their professional services.

A young orderly, who worked in burn ward of Brooke Army Medical Center, was a profound scholar, a champion swimmer and athlete, who wore his talents humbly. This young man, according to the officer in charge of the research unit, was inducted into the service of his country as a ward aide when he could have had a much higher rank. He possessed an attribute of kindness that seemed to reach out to all those sick and suffering boys in the ward. He comforted and visited with each boy as he worked, so that a serenity and happiness seemed to settle over the ward and permeate the room whenever he entered.

Then, too, another young orderly and a nurse seemed filled with this same God-given power of spreading tranquility among those whose bodies were so filled with pain.

Kindness did not stop with the nurses, doctors, and orderlies. Even the other patients showed how truly great the capacity for compassion among men can be. A Cerebral Palsy Telethon drive was in progress at the time. One of the boys, who was gravely ill, started a collection and asked if I would take it to the program. The boys, who could ill-afford such generosity, together, gave a good sum of money; some gave all they had. How wonderful it was to see the happiness on their faces. As they were assisting others, they became entirely unmindful of their own misfortunes.

Even the youngsters got in on the act of helping. One young friend of our son Bill was a professional juvenile performer with a popular band. During the latter part of my husband's hospital confinement, he and Bill came into the burn ward as entertainers. The friend with his guitar and Bill with his saxophone played and sang for the patients in the burn ward and truly brightened their day .

Of course, my precious mother was always there for us and never stopped loving, helping, and sacrificing for us then, as well as, for years to come.

My brothers, who are building contractors, set about rebuilding our home; many people offered their help, and other businessmen offered materials for rebuilding.

Many people provided emotional support and many offered their services. With emotions out of control and confusion in control, I didn't know how to begin to deal with my anguished feelings, but someone did, and I was especially blessed when she became my frequent companion and confidant.

During my darkest hours when I had not the strength nor composure to respond to visitors, my cousin whose child had died of cystic fibrosis sat quietly beside the bed. She willingly shared her time, empathy, and experience to provide invaluable support and understanding.

She along with other fellow sufferers who had experienced tragic loss themselves, knew that grieving alone denies needed support and leads to depression. They helped me understand that an emotion not claimed can't be expressed, and dealt with. They taught me not to deny, but to acknowledge my honest emotions and release them through talking, crying. That is to say, they taught me to lessen the pain through sharing my feelings of apprehension, panic, confusion, pain, guilt, and resentment.

My cousin offered, "When you need someone to listen or to cry with, call me or someone you trust. Please, don't hide your pain and grieve alone. If you do, you are not dealing with it, and unresolved grief often causes serious emotional problems in the future." She also did those practical things which she, from experience, knew so well needed to be done: buying stamps, making lists, sending thank-you notes, and graciously accommodating our out-of-town relatives in her home.

For many months she continued emotional support, companionship, and practical help. She accompanied me to the cemetery and other places that were difficult to approach, and telephoned or visited on the special days that she knew would be painful.

She recognized my mother's grief, brought her gifts that said, "I understand that you too are grieving, and I care about you." She periodically called Mother, took her out, supported and encouraged her.

My sister, perceptive of our needs, requested that our boys stay together in her home for the remainder of the school year. She gave them attention, security and love so necessary to their recovery. She not only provided for their physical needs, but also sensed their need for reassurance. She and a friend provided ongoing communication and involved the boys in such things as helping pack and temporarily store the remaining family belongings and allowed them to take part in decision-making.

Concerned about Bill's internal grief with only silent tears to release his hidden feelings, she initiated conversations with him and found that both boys were blaming themselves for not being able to rescue Dianne and David. Giving them many opportunities to express their feelings and ask questions, she provided the repetitious reassurance that was so necessary.

In an effort to minimize their trauma and apprehension, many concerned people supplied hugs, and since the boys were a great consolation to each other, they involved both boys in family and community activities. Steve said, "Mom, I don't think we could have made it those first days if we had been separated from each other. We really needed to be together."

Many people showed a sensitivity to the needs of our sons as well as to us. Although parents of a small child, my husband's brother and his wife drove from Dallas to San Antonio each weekend to sit with my husband and give us moral support. When the school year ended, they then took Steve to Dallas to spend the summer with them. My sister-in-law took Bill to Arkansas for awhile.

Friends as well as both our families were generous, thoughtful and helpful. Depressing and difficult times were made easier by two loving friends, who when my husband went back to work came to be with me and brought with them whatever work they had to do. They came each day until I could begin to face the future with hope.

A friend who had never had the child of

her heart's desire reached out to comfort me. The pain and tears of empathy and understanding in her eyes reflected a tragedy that was momentarily greater than mine and brought needed wisdom that changed my attitude of bitterness to one of thankfulness for our *Borrowed Joy.*

Although God was and is our heavenly strength, our family and friends have supplied our earthly fortitude. The warmth and care that we received not only helped us but radiated and spread its ripples to help relieve the misery and suffering of others.

Priceless Gifts

by
Della Pylant

I. Help? Let Me Count the Ways!
II. Reaching Out to Others
III. Reaching Out to Children and Teens

In hope of reaching as many hurting people as possible, sections of this book have been reproduced for organizations and support groups. Therefore short exerpts necessarily are repeated from one section to another.

The **Borrowed Joy** section has also been reproduced in booklet form. These booklets are available only to organizations and support groups. FAX, telephone, or write the publisher on organization letterhead to request information on quantity purchases.

Warning Disclaimer

Not an ultimate source, this book is designed to provide experiential information to complement, amplify, and supplement other information on the subject. The publisher and author are **not** rendering professional services. For **expert assistance seek a competent professional.**

Effort has been made to provide accurate information, but **mistakes in content and typography are possible.**

The author and the publisher shall have neither liability nor responsibility for any loss or damage caused, or alleged to be caused, directly or indirectly by the information contained in this book.

If you do not wish to be bound by the above, you may return this book to publisher for full refund.

Reaching Out to Others

by
Della Pylant

Reaching Out To Others

Emotional support and care as well as practical assistance are revealed in the following conversation between this survivor and a survivor-caregiver who had earlier experienced her own little son's battle with Cystic Fibrosis and his ensuing death.

Disclosed are many examples of the support that is vital to recovery and sometimes even to the life of survivors of tragedy and pain.

Revealed also in the dialog are many innovative ways care givers use their own particular talents, creativity, or adeptness to give practical assistance, assistance which provides comfort and preserves the energy of the bereaved and closely related family members who are also grieving and need remembrance.

The conversation portrays examples of monetary and business assistance. These acts alleviated some of the added stress brought on the family by a fire that destroyed their home and took the lives of two precious children, a beautiful little five-year-old girl and her eleven-month-old baby brother.

"You know, Charline, following tragic loss or death, wonderfully caring people often contribute support to survivors; some, emotional support, others, monetary or practical help. Still others want to help but are intimidated by lack of knowledge or experience. I understand reluctance to go to grieving people and risk saying or doing the wrong thing and causing more pain."

"I, too, understand because I had those same feelings. I could think of no words that were sufficient or even effective, and after experiencing my own child's death, I know that words fail completely during those first hours of shock. Yet, I don't know how I could have survived without my friends and family.

They were the support that held our lives together. Your experience reinforced my awareness of the vital significance of support from family and friends."

"Oh you bet! Yet, I can understand the intimidation of those who have never experienced the needs demanded by intense grief nor learned how to approach a bereaved person."

"Yes, I understand that too; it's such an emotional time for everyone involved. I remember so well that the first hours I spent with you after the fire brought back so many emotions and reinforced my awareness of the vital influence of momentous support from family and friends. I wish everyone wouldn't worry about what to say. I wish they knew that the words that reach the pain better than any others are, 'I love you; I care!'

But concern is legitimate because many times the words that are said do cause pain. Not understanding the survivors' need for someone to listen and allow them to talk about the deceased, loving and caring people in an attempt to comfort say things that encourage survivors to grieve alone. Then they are puzzled at the reaction of the survivors."

"You are right. I recall the anguish of a wife whose husband had died. She was devastated because family members and friends avoided talking about the death or even mentioning it.

She came from another town to visit her family. Not understanding her need and wishing to ease her pain, they planned activities to distract her thoughts to other things. They sensed her intense pain, and were concerned about her seemingly growing hostility toward them. Her mother and sister suggested they go shopping and were very puzzled at her outburst of bitter emotions and early departure from her visit.

Terminally ill and concerned about her daughter, this mother wanted to meet her daughter's needs but did not know how. She asked me if I could help her daughter.

On the daughter's next visit, I invited them to lunch. At the table tension and apprehension were pervasive.

I said to the daughter, 'I was so sorry to hear of your husband's death.'

Very emotionally she said, 'I'm glad you care enough to talk about it. My family certainly doesn't '

She apologized as she began to weep.

I said 'No, don't apologize, crying is okay. It doesn't embarrass me. If you need to cry, please do. Crying and talking are the ways we can deal with our pain, and this is more important than concern for people around us.'

She said, 'Oh, thank you! I do need to talk about him and know that others are remembering him and caring. My family and friends don't talk to me about him and his death or even acknowledge that it happened.

Some of the people at work act as though nothing has happened, and others pass me and barely speak as if they are afraid.

I feel so much pain because it seems as if in their minds, he doesn't and never did exist. That hurts so badly. I need them to show that they care and remember him and his death.

In trying to deal with this I have been reading books that say good can come from pain, but I certainly don't see any good.

I have gone to church, but I don't get the comfort I need. Would you believe the pastor asked me to serve on the bereavement committee?'

I said, 'Yes, I would. Who more than one who has experienced the death of a loved one could better empathize and form a bond with another going through a similar experience. The sharing can help bring comfort and healing to you, as well as the person you reach out to.'

She said, 'That's true, and I never thought about it like that. I, too, could have been comforted by someone who had experienced what I was going through. I think the reason you can help me now is because you have suffered too.'

I answered, 'Yes, and do you realize that you just spoke to a point you raised earlier? You just told me some good that came from my pain. You told me that is why I can help you. That's a choice we have. Helping others also helps our own healing; whereas, becoming bitter devastates and hurts.

Your friends at work really do care, and your family certainly cares very much, but they, as many others, have never been trained to know how to help people in pain. They want to help and comfort you but are afraid they will cause more pain by saying the wrong thing or even by mentioning your husband's name or his death.'

'Do they think that I will stop thinking about him because they don't talk about him?'

'No, but their fears are probably about their own ability to comfort, and that causes them to avoid facing the issue with you or other grieving people. They, just as I once did, probably think they have to say something that will take away or lessen the agony, when of course that really isn't possible. They don't understand that you need them to listen and let you, the hurting person, do the talking. Therefore, you have some responsibility too, to help them understand. If family members don't mention his name, you can do it. Tell them, [I need to talk. I need you to listen. I need to know that you share my feelings and to have you tell me that you care.]

Need I say tears were shed and progress begun toward recovery?"

"Della, as you were talking, I could picture that happening. I really wish everyone could understand that a priority need of the grieving person is to share the grief and release some of the pain through communication."

"Oh yes! I'm so thankful that I wasn't

left to grieve alone. I had been trying to be very private and sophisticated in my grief by not showing emotions publicly I was becoming an absolute powerless zombie with one part after another of my existence falling away. The force that had moved in and split our family with death, injury and division with each separation took away a part of me.

Confusion continued to control. I knew I needed to make decisions and do things that were harder than I had ever done, but I could no longer define my role nor make decisions. The apprehension and pain were so intense that even breathing seemed difficult, but thank God, you and others encouraged me to talk and acknowledge these emotions and deal with them. The more I talked about the children and their death and talked about and dealt with my feelings , the less frequently I needed to talk about them. I may never have dealt with my feelings honestly, had you not helped me to understand and encouraged me and listened.

I'll always be grateful that you were

there to hug me and cry with me and listen to me as I struggled through the shock and disbelief after Dianne and David's death. I'm not sure I would have recovered or perhaps even survived without your help. The painful emotions displaced all values and logic and reason."

"My earlier experience helps me understand your needs, and assisting you is part of my own healing. I'm glad I could be there for you and can be here for you now."

"Oh yes! I know now that your being there to listen and encourage me was what I needed most, and I'm thankful I had supportive family and friends. Shock, pain and confusion crowded out all control and paralyzed my ability to reason. Emotional support from family and friends was probably vital to my life. The pain was so intense that even breathing seemed difficult, but thank God you were there for me.

I remember the first day I was home from

the hospital and not able to receive any visitors yet but turning over and seeing you sitting there beside my bed. You said, 'I'm here for you if you want to talk. If you don't, that's okay. I'll sit here with you, or if you want to be alone, I'll go into the other room with your mom.'"

"I thought that no one could understand what I was feeling, but that you did understand was becoming apparent and was comforting. I recall thinking, 'She too has suffered through the death of a child.' You didn't say the things that some well-meaning people were saying, things that you or I may once have said, things that made me know they couldn't possibly understand what I was feeling. You didn't say, 'Don't cry!' You cried with me. You didn't say, 'Don't talk about it; it makes you feel worse.' You knew that I needed to talk, and you listened. You didn't say, 'You do have other children.' You understood that each life is wonderfully intricate and precious and one can never replace another."

"Della, I knew that nothing I could say would help when you were experiencing the agonizing initial shock, denial, and disbelief, but I felt that because of our kindred spirits, we could draw strength from each other."

"Well, I know that your presence gave me added emotional strength that I needed desperately. Because painful emotions alone were in control, comfort came not from words, but only through loving support that reached through to the pain. That support came from you and from the touch of a friend's hand on mine and from the warm embraces that touched my pain with their comfort and from the shared grief of sincere tears that gave me the freedom to cry and release some of the pain.

Not only through your tears did you share my grief, but you spoke to my immediate need. When questions with no answers bombarded my brain, you listened with empathy and without judgement while I vented my anger and bitterness. You never tried to avoid or change the subject.

You seemed to understand that time alone would not heal, but that time along with support and knowledge would bring faith and recovery. Your listening brought release of bad feelings and began the healing so necessary for my bruised and trampled emotions."

"Yes, having a trusted listener is a vital part of recovery, and do you also understand that your sharing your pain with me is part of my recovery? Having experienced similar pain, I have the same needs."

"Forgive me, I needed to be reminded of that. Sometimes I wonder how you could have been so patient with me. You must have tired of my over and over again telling the details of the tragedy and related incidents. Do you remember that talking about them became easier. Each time talking brought remembrance of forgotten incidents and feelings, feelings that you encouraged me to examine and to deal with?"

"Yes, I do remember. Repetition is part of

recovery. I wish every care giver knew the significance of patient, non-judgemental listening."

"Nothing brings release of pain and confusion more than talking to a trusted and patient listener. You not only listened, but you were at ease using your son Michael's name as well as Dianne and David's.

Earlier when I had tried to talk about them, I became a screaming maniac again, but as you courageously used their names and talked about happier times with your children and mine, you validated characteristics of my children that brought both pain and joy. But finally, I could ventilate my emotions, find reality, let go of the pain and find comfort in memories that became and remain a part of our lives."

"Oh yes! When you could talk about Dianne and David without sobbing, I knew you had begun to recover."

"Oh! I ran the complete gamut of human

emotions after the tragedy, but your perceptive questions helped me sort out invalid feelings of guilt and apprehension and reach the truth."

"I, too, still have to be guarded because those feelings pop up for me as well. I wonder whether or not I should have done more. Michael needed consistent attention to lessen the ravages of his fatal disease, and sometimes my thoughts were self accusations. When those thoughts come, I've learned to examine them, accept any real guilt, and forgive myself just as I forgive others. Since we are imperfect human beings and become weary and discouraged, we are bound to fall short sometimes no matter how hard we try. Most times the guilt feelings are not valid. Sometimes, however, memories play tricks and bring delusions of guilt."

"Oh yes, they do, but you had to deal with a task of love and responsibility that was as unending as your pain as you watched your child struggle for breath so many times. Yet your patience and devotion to him were foremost. Only God could have supplied the courage to keep on keeping on when you knew the inevitable end.

For a long time I hurt when I remembered that Dianne had wanted to come to the car the second time when I was leaving for my brother's home the day of the fire. I had stopped once to reassure her, hug and kiss her, but then I sent her into the house where her dad was. I have wished a million times I could feel those little arms around my neck and see her precious smile and hear her giggle and take the tiny rosebuds from her beautiful little hands.

I admire you so much, and I thank God for you and what you've done for me, my mom. and my family. More and more memories are comforting, and I'm learning to deal positively with those negative times and get on with living and caring for my family. Words can never express my thanks for the emotional as well as the practical support from you and many others.

Not only an abundance of emotional support but practical help as well was extended to my family, and comfort comes with remembrance of those kindnesses and the great tact and sensitivity taken to not intrude nor overwhelm. I understand that offers of help were so abundant that eventually some had to be refused. The generous, empathic friends who offered help seemed very sensitive to our feelings and needs and seemed not to be offended when told that our needs had been amply fulfilled.

I truly hope that no one took the refusal personally because we appreciated the offers, but many resources existed within our own family and close friends."

"Yes, the offer of help is comforting. Rejection of help should not be taken personally. Personalities differ. Some have great difficulty accepting help, and some are extremely private."

"Charline, your practical help showed a

very special sensitivity. Your supplying trans-
portation and accommodations in your home
exhibited your graciousness and uncommon
thoughtfulness. You kept lists, shopped, sent
notes, bought stamps and did so many things
that from experience you knew needed to be
done."

"Well, not only I, but so many of your
friends felt your pain and had a need to share.
You had helped others, and now many people
were touched by the sudden catastrophic tragedy of your children's death, your husband's
injuries, and the loss of your home. Now they
were asking your family members, friends,
and neighbors for information about your
current needs. Their way of sharing your pain
was to give financial help and to relieve your
grieving family members of routine tasks, as
well as those peculiar to the time. The inquir-
ers and those they represented offered help in
numerous ways: telephoning, errands, child
care for your extended family, pet care, lawn
and flower care, car service, food preparation
and service.

Knowledgeable volunteers (with some counsel and guidance from a key family member) answered the door, received guests, relayed messages about arrangements and preferred tributes, kept lists, shopped, sent notes, organized volunteer services, and made the necessary telephone calls, (including local and long distance relatives, church, work places and schools of family members).

Warm meals were served to the family and buffet meals were set up for out of town family members. Fresh flowers were sent to the home before and after services. These thoughtful courtesies conserved the energy and emotions of family members."

"Truly, people from near and far did seem anxious to share with us not only their sympathy but their resources as well. Thanks for remembering those things with me. The care and thoughtfulness behind all those acts certainly encouraged us.

Grief doesn't end quickly and the need for

support escalates during the weeks and months following major loss. Your continued support was and is part of our progressive recovery. Your telephone calls, invitations, visits, remembrance on birthdays and holidays are consolations that say, 'I am standing by for you; I know that full recovery is ahead, and I'm here.'"

"That is true. When people aren't around all the time, thoughts and grief become accelerated. Depression can overwhelm as it did you when you were handling and disposing of David and Dianne's personal effects."

"Oh, yes, that severance devastatingly stabbed at the bonding I had shared with my children. That painful task should never be rushed. I'm glad no one pushed me to do it before experience taught me the pain I was bringing on myself by making idols of possessions. Support from a close family member was an absolute necessity to help and encourage me to think clearly and make decisions. I was the only one to truly know when the time was right, which effects were to go, and to whom or where. Even though very difficult, decisions about their personal effects could be made only by me."

"I agree, but decisions became so debilitating to you that at one point, you couldn't continue."

"I had to stop several times and get my emotions under control, and then I would get back to the difficult decisions after taking some time for thought. When decisions became too painful and parting with certain items unbearable, I kept those items, and now, they are momentos of comfort."

"Comfort comes from a variety of sources as does pain. Disposing of the deceased's clothes requires careful consideration. Perhaps they should be given to one who will not be wearing them in the presence of the survivors. Others may find, as you did, that unexpectedly seeing another wear the deceased's clothing can be shockingly traumatic, especially, if worn by one of similar body build and coloring."

"The unexpectedness of that incident and the the little girl's close resemblance to Dianne caused the shock. If I had been prepared and been expecting it, possibly I would have handled it better.

Charline, you were not only my care giver but also my model for reaching out to help ease the pain of others, as you are doing for me."

"That's great! That means you become a model for those you comfort. Hopefully, rather than grieve alone, survivors will make their needs known and receive support that will help them face the future with hope."

"I echo those hopes. I hope survivors will learn to say, 'I understand that you don't know what to say and that's okay, but please don't avoid me or pass me by. Spend a little time with me, give me a hug, or squeeze my hand. Through your presence I will feel your care. Please find time to let me talk and if I cry or you cry, don't be disturbed. You don't have to hold up for me. You will be sharing my grief.'

I also pray that, with their hearts, care givers will hear this message from the bereaved even when it is unspoken. The personal gain that comes from the non-judgmental listening comes not just from vicariously sharing the pain but from sharing the recovery as well."

Reaching Out

to Children

and Teenagers

by Della Pylant

(Experiential

Observations)

Warning Disclaimer

Not an ultimate source, this book is designed to provide experiential information to complement, amplify, and supplement other information on the subject. The publisher and author are **not** rendering professional services. For **expert assistance seek a competent professional.**

Effort has been made to provide accurate information, but **mistakes in content and typography are possible.**

The author and the publisher shall have neither liability nor responsibility for any loss or damage caused, or alleged to be caused, directly or indirectly by the information contained in this book.

If you do not wish to be bound by the above, you may return this book to publisher for full refund.

Reaching Out to Children and Teens

"Mom, we were hurting so much we couldn't have made it if we weren't together. We knew Sister was hurt, and they were trying to save her. We thought they couldn't, but we didn't know . . . we didn't know. We didn't know for sure about David. We thought Daddy died, and we knew you were in the hospital. We didn't know if you were goin' to die. We needed to see you and be with you. We didn't know what was going to happen or where we'd live if you were gone too. We felt so scared and lonely. We cried and cried and promised each other, 'No matter what, we'll stay t'gether, and we'll make it some way.' I was so glad Bill was with me. We cried and cried; it was so hard. We thought we should've gotten Sister and David out before they got hurt. Mom, why did they have to die?"

Statement was from eight-year-old Steve after his little sister and baby brother died in a tragic fire, and his father lay critically burned in an army burn center.

When our sons needed prompt information, answers, and family participation, we parents were debilitated by shock, grief, and injury. Impaired by our own emotional and physical stress, we who represented their security could not supply our sons' needs. They looked on in horror at the scene on their front lawn where rescue workers tried in vain to save their little sister and brother and then turned to see their parents rushed away in shrieking ambulances flashing danger warnings.

Bill and Steve, shocked, frightened, and bewildered, were taken by a patrolman friend to the safe and shielded environment of my sister's home. At the scene earlier, they had seen and heard that their dad was very badly burned, but no information nor answers were available to the boys for some time. What they imagined was more frightening than reality. They believed their whole family was dead.

When information did come, the family, feeling the boys had been through too much trauma and didn't need added pain, shielded them from bad news, but they sensed that they were not being told complete truth, and this frightened them because in their minds things too bad to talk about must be the very worst.

When they went back to school, they picked up rumors and inaccurate fragments and exaggerations from their peers who had overheard adult conversations. This added to their doubt, apprehension, and insecurity and heightened their need for complete and honest information.

That they were less apprehensive when they received complete and prompt information became obvious. At times the news was indeed dark and dismal until their Dad's skin grafts were complete. However, when they were kept informed and knew what to expect, they discussed it and helped each other prepare to deal with it. They began to trust that they would receive early and accurate information as soon as it was available

Later, when I could be with them for short periods of time, Steve said, "Mom, in the beginning we didn't know who was telling us the truth, so we didn't really know what was happening." He asked questions, talked, and cried. Afraid of hurting me more, he was reluctant to ask the most painful questions about his little sister. Both boys feared that their questions would cause more pain. Deferring to my need, they grieved silently without having answers to some of their questions. I learned that nothing was more painful and frightening to them than not knowing.

As older children and teenagers often do, Bill, twelve years old, quiet and reticent felt that he had to be "brave" and "courageous" and not show his emotions. He had tried to keep his grief inside and vent his emotions only when he was alone.

Hearing of my sister's concern about Bill's silence and his tears, a skilled and sensitive friend who understood Bill's need asked relevant questions and encouraged him to talk about his feelings and ask questions. Apprehension and fears began to surface when the friend listened and answered his questions.

Sensitively listening for clues that would reveal Bill's need, this perceptive friend began, first, to help with the troubled thoughts and then to supply information and pose apt questions to help both Bill and Steve deal with reality and find their own answers. "What do you think happened?" "Was it really possible for you to save your little sister or brother?" "What stopped you?" "How could you have done it?" "Did someone else do it?" "Why not?" "So, no one could've saved them, huh?"

With help Bill began to understand that effective recovery is not done alone, that hiding feelings is not "brave" but destructive. Finally he understood that unless he expressed his grief, he couldn't deal with it and could become emotionally ill. As difficult as it was, he shared his pain and acknowledged and dealt with the excruciating reality of loss.

Since the security of home, siblings, and parents was suddenly swept away, our sons questioned the consequences and the future. They needed repetitive reassurance that they would not be left alone, that they would be cared for and have all their needs met. They needed to know about plans and provisions and to have frequent information about us, their parents, and about the support people who would be caring for them and transporting them while we were not available. They were insecure when information was withheld.

Keeping them together when they were in a new environment lessened trauma and allowed the boys comfort of companionship with each other. According to them adding separation to their loss and displacement would have made pain and apprehension unbearable. Keeping as nearly as possible their accustomed routine, my sister provided an environment that was conducive to communication.

When they were encouraged to help plan and make decisions about food, personal hygiene, and appropriate clothes, they talked together and made good decisions, and began to feel some control over their lives again. By sharing tasks with their aunt, they curbed loneliness and exchanged information. Included in preparations and plans, they set expectations for themselves and gained self direction. When my sister's lady friend who had helped the boys pack remaining family belongings also helped them deal with feelings of sadness, fear, and anger, the boys could better direct their actions and behavior constructively. As she listened to them, she reinforced the concept that these are natural, appropriate feelings that we all must deal with.

Through research and listening to parents, counselors, psychiatrists, and psychologists, as well as, to many children and adults who had experienced tragedy in their youth, I learned that children and teenagers release tension in different ways. Their laughter may be an autonomous response to tension. Their yells and angry remarks may be reaction to an overwhelming sense of guilt (imagined or real) that makes children feel so unacceptable that they hide their feelings and release pain through unusual behavior.

To dispel such fears, children urgently need acceptance and love, regardless of the behavior. First, they need to understand that nothing other people think or say causes the death of another. They can then be helped to claim and resolve guilt (valid or invalid). Our sons felt that somehow they should have rescued Dianne and David and needed to understand that nothing they could have done or said would have stopped the death. Continued communication and our friend's apt questions helped the boys recognize that their painful feelings were not valid. They also understood that if guilt is valid, we claim it and know that we all make mistakes for which we must forgive ourselves. The boys learned that bitter feelings shut out comfort and breed cynicism and sarcasm.

Often skilled, understanding friends who have experienced similar feelings themselves help youngsters resolve bad feelings; yet some of them require a professional to help sort out irrational feelings of guilt or fear.

A very dangerous form of guilt comes from a child's invalid belief that he or she should have been the one to die because the deceased was more loved or more important to the parent or to the world. A beautiful young adult friend is an example of how devastating this burden can be. She did not resolve her invalid feelings of guilt and unworthiness but carried them into adult life. She took her life.

To help him say goodbye to his sister, Steve wrote letters and drew pictures to express unfinished plans, wishes, and broken dreams. Dianne's cousin expressed painful feelings through drawing pictures and then telling about the picture. A care giver used puppet interaction to help her say goodbye. The puppets could say things too painful for her to say.

Bill and Steve began to openly talk and shed tears after an admired and respected uncle, without embarrassment, openly expressed his feelings. They needed a model to show them that life moves on and to understand that talking, crying, and expressing emotions are healthy ways to expess grief. Their uncle, in the middle of grief, played and laughed with them and showed pleasure in things non-related to the death. The boys then felt comfortable and began to relax.

Our sons were encouraged to recall memories of pleasant times with Dianne and David. Their cousin talked about Dianne and David's memorable characteristics that would have a continued effect on us the survivors. She encouraged our sons to recall pleasant memories and ask the questions that were in their minds. They found the freedom to voice memories of happy times with their sister and brother. They found peace of mind when questions about the present and future state-of-being of Dianne and David were answered honestly. Happy memories and anticipation that one day they would see their brother and sister again helped them say good-bye. Although a long and tough struggle still lay ahead during their father's readjustment and extended recovery, the boys had taken time to resolve their grief and accomplish their goodbyes, and they began to move forward with their lives.

When someone said, "Bill, you can be the man in the house until your Dad is well," admittedly, I was troubled. I had several times seen the folly of a surviving parent, who when the other left or died expected a teenager to take responsibilities of the missing parent or expected one child to take the place of another who had died. Although former life styles may have to change drastically, every human being has the right to his or her own role and self identity.

Neither a relationship nor a life can be replaced. Adding emotional or physical stress to a child or teenager's grief is not only unfair but sometimes unbearable. After severe loss children need not only freedom from stress but also continued understanding and support as well.

Children usually grieve severely and sometimes have guilt feelings when they lose contact with a parent through separation, be it from death, divorce, foreign service, abuse or other reason. These children need emotional support and understanding.

Since youngsters identify with both parents as a part of themselves, the absent parent should not be spoken of negatively. When either parent is severely belittled, the child, seeing himself or herself as a part of that parent, also feels belittled.

Two of my teenage students from different families grew solemn and lost much of their confidence. The parents had divorced, and the fathers were alienated from the family. These adolescent boys needed identity with and longed for a relationship with their fathers. They wanted so much to see the fathers even if contact came just once a year. They had heard many negative things about this person who was validation of their own existence. Having been told that their fathers were no good and didn't care about them was destructive to the boys self value. Whether or not it was true is not the point. They felt that they themselves must not be of much value if their own fathers couldn't love them nor care about them.

These middle school students were both very lovable, gentle and handsome boys with ability to do well; yet both took drugs to escape the pain of feeling unwanted by their fathers. One of the boys told me that he had seen his father for the first time in several years when the father who was a big handsome long haul truck driver had come through the city and contacted him. He said, "I look like him. More than anything I wanted to be with him! I just wanted to know him better! When he told me that I coundn't spend a little bit of time with him at his home, I asked him to let me be with him on the ride back to California and then I could take the bus or plane back home. I would have given anything to be with him! He cried, but he didn't let me! It hurts!"

Without someone to listen and share their

pain and reassure them of their own self worth, these children found life unbearable. Looking for their own self-identity, they felt a great unending loss too difficult to deal with. They stopped working or caring about their grades. They became lethargic and ambivilent as if it were safer not to feel anything.

However, they did better when they talked about their feelings and received reassurance that we don't know the circumstances behind the father's actions or what has happened to cause his problems. I assured the boys that each of them was a wonderfully intricate human being with the capacity for doing great things, that each was here for a very special reason and could contribute much to the world and could have a wonderful life ahead by making the right choices now.

Pointing out their individual strong qualities and talents helped bolster their confidence. I tried to help them understand that even though they couldn't control some of the things that were happening to them, they did have a choice. They could either let those circumstances control and take them down, or they could take control of their lives and do the things that would help them achieve what they wanted in the future and perhaps one day get to know their father. These thoughts helped them gain some sense of control and responsibility to make positive choices.

Children can feel so much better about themselves and their future if instead of hearing negative things about an absent parent, they can hear about positive plans for the future and hear the parent who is present say, "None of this is your fault, and this is not something we wanted to happen. But because we as parents can't get along together doesn't mean that either of us is bad or doesn't love you. Sometimes people have very different temperaments and just can't make it together. It's okay for you to feel bad about it. We all do, but we are going to get on with our life, and together with God's help we will make it a good one "

If the parent is under stress and unable to supply this care, timely listening and loving care from an unobtrusive and sensitive teacher, friend or relative can be invaluable and let the children know that someone is available for them.

Many people helped our sons survive trauma and become fine young men. Without that momentous support and help at a critical time in their lives, they may have borne intense scars for a lifetime. Listening, loving, inquiring, writing, telephoning, inviting, and visiting were remembrances that said to them, "I acknowledge and understand that you are grieving. I am standing by."

Victory

Oh Tragedy! Companion of bitterness!
You burn with fire, kill with gun and blade.
Rob future and present of victims' touch.
Confusion and darkness are your trade.
A mother's heart bleeds and hurts so much
Life cannot continue without relief!
Help! Help me, God! Help my unbelief.

You were there, God, to hear my shout
To quiet my anguish and dispel my doubt,
To teach me what life is truly about.
That our pain need not go unheeded.
For we recognize pain in eyes of another,
And in sharing find healing we have needed.
In reaching out and helping each other.

With warm embraces we give comfort,
With tender hearts we share the tears,
With listening ears we release the pain.
As fellow victims we expose the fears,
Claim the grief and deal with the pain.
By reaching out in love and giving,
We return the gift of peaceful living.

PHOTOS

(Most family pictures were destroyed or damaged in the fire. All of little David's pictures were destroyed.)

Fun in
Uncle
Albert's
jeep

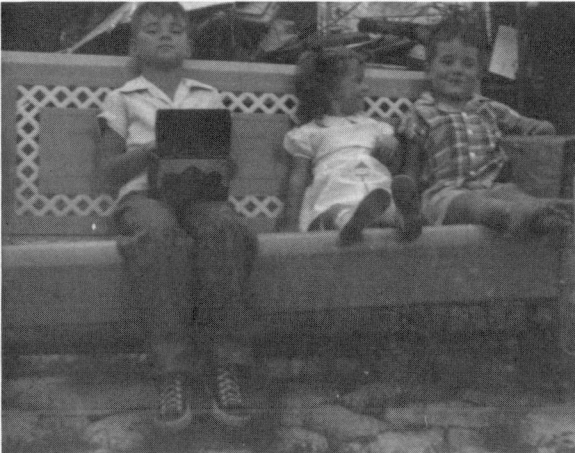

Music buff Bill entertains Dianne and Steve

Dianne
and
Grandpa
Pylant

Aunt Bev
and
Dianne

The
family
at the
zoo

Christmas dinner at Mamo's house

Steve and Dianne - favorite playmates

"Santa, please bring Dianne a walking doll."

Dianne and Bill

Dianne

Christmas Act Helps
Mother Forget Tragedy

Mrs. B. J. Pylant will not see joy of Christmas on the faces of two of her children again. But Mrs. Pylant has a project that helps her forget this sorrow; she has baked some 12 dozen cookies, spending hours decorating them colorfully as trees, angels and other holiday symbols. She takes them in gaily wrapped packages to the children in Baptist Memorial Hospital's children's ward.

The San Antonio woman began her "cookie" mission because she thought "doing little things for other people" would help her get over a tragic fire which claimed the lives of two of her children.

Mrs. Pylant and her husband were severely burned and a daughter, Dianne, then 5, and a son, David, 11 months, died. Though Mrs. Pylant has a new son this Christmas, born in August, and two older sons to care for, she found time to bake, decorate and deliver the cookies to the hospital. A friend, Mrs. J. A. Bingham, helped decorate the cookies.

The young mother said the kindness of friends, neighbors and relatives, including help in rebuilding the family home and donations to pay for the childrens' funerals, showed her how helpful friends can be. She wanted to find a way to help others, too.

She said, "I am the one who receives the blessing when I bake these cookies."

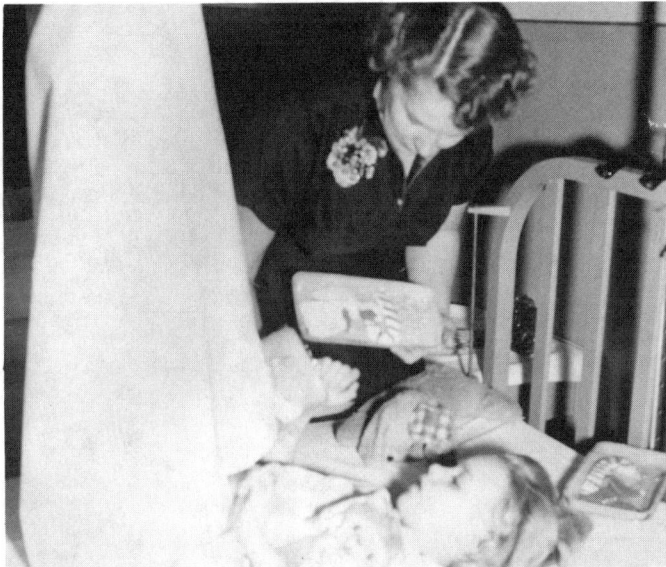

COOKIE MISSION — Little Kay Alexander admires cookie Santa, tree, and star, baked and colorfully decorated by Mrs. B. J. Pylant. Connie is one of Baptist Memorial Hospital children's ward patients to receive some 12 dozen cookies distributed by Mrs. Pylant Friday. — Staff Photo

Bibliography

Agee, James. *A Death in the Family*. New
York: Avon Books, 1959.

Arms, Suzanne.*To Love and Let Go*. New
York: Alfred A. Knopf, 1983.

Bayly, Joseph.*The Last Thing We Talk
About*. Elgin, IL: David C. Cook
Publishing Co., 1973.

Becker, Earnest. *The Denial of Death*. New
York: The Free Press, 1973.

Billheimer, Paul E. *Destined for the Throne*.
Minneapolis:Bethany House Publishers,
1975.

Bishop, Joseph. *The Eye of the Storm*.
Minneapolis: Bethany House Publishers, 1976.

Carmichael, Amy. *ROSE FROM BRIAR*.
Fort Washington, Pennsylvania: CLC.
1933.

Cato, Sid. *Healing Life's Great Hurts*.
Chicago: Chicago Review Press, 1973.

Donnelly, Katherine. *Recovering from the
Loss of a Child*. NY: MacMillan
Publishing, 1982.

Grollman, Earl A. *Talking about Death-A Dialogue Between Parent and Child.* Boston: Beacon Press,1970.

Gunther, John. Death Be Not Proud. New York: Harper & Rowe, 1949.

Henry, Iona and Frank S. Mead. *Triumph over Tragedy.* Westwood, NJ: Fleming H. Revell Co., 1957.

Knapp, Ronald. *Beyond Endurance*: *When a Child Dies.* New York: Shocken Books, 1986.

Kostenbaum, Peter. *Is There an Answer to Death?* Englewood Cliffs, N.J.: Prentice-Hall, 1975.

Kreis, Bernadine, and Alice Pattie. *Up from Grief Patterns of Recovery.* Minneapolis: The Seabury Press. 1969.

Kubler-Ross, Elizabeth. *Death: The Final Stage of Growth.* Englewood Cliffs, N.J.: Prentice Hall, 1975.

_____. *On Death and Dying.* New York: Alfred A. Knopf, 1981.

_____. *To Live Until We Say Good-bye.* Fnglewood Cliffs, N.J.: Prentice-Hall, 1978.

Kushner, Harold. *When Bad Things Happen to Good People*. New York: Avon Books, 1983.

Lewis,C. S. *A Grief Observed*. New York: Bantam SeaburyPress, 1963.

Price, Eugenia. *Getting Through the Night*. New York: Random House, 1983.

Rando, Therese A. *Parental Loss of a Child*. Champaign, IL: Research Press, 1980.

Reed, Elizabeth. *Helping Children Through the Mystery of Death*. Nashville: Abbington Press, 1970.

Rosen, Helen. *Unspoken Grief-Coping with Childhood Sibling Loss*. Rutgers, NJ: Lexington Books, 1986.

Rudolph, Marguerita. *Should Children Know?* New York: Shocken Books Inc., 1978.

Schiff, Harriet Sarnoff. *The Bereaved Parent*. New York: Crown Publishers, Inc., 1977

Swindol, Chuck. *For those who hurt*. Portland: Multnomah Press, 1984.

Vogel, Linda Jane. *Helping a Child Understand Death.* Philadelphia: Fortress
Press, 1975.

Vredevelt, Pam W. *Empty Arms.* Portland:
Multnomah Press,1984.

Wanderer, Zev. *Letting Go.* New York:
Warner Books, 1978.

Westberg. Granger E. *Good Grief.* Philadelphia: Fortress Press, 1962.

Interviews and Lectures

Allen, Jimmy, Ph.D.

Edens, David, M.D. Psychologist

Elmore, Vernon, D.D.

Gorsuch, Paul. M. D. Oncologist,
Surgeon, Bible Teacher.

Haygood, B. Thomas Ph.D. Sociology

Jennings, James. M.D. Psychiatrist

Koop, Charles, M. D. Surgeon General

Lucenay, Harry L., D.D.

McMillan, J. Grant, D. D.

Orozco, Carlos, M.D.

Schaeffer, Francis, Ph. D.

Siever, James. M.D., Gyn/Ob

Sylvester, David, Ph. D.

Walker, David, D.D.

Zuschlag, Ella, M.D. Pediatrician

All the many fellow grievers who
shared their painful experiences

VICTORY
OVER
! Tragedy !

Heavenly strength,

Earthly fortitude,

Tender hearts,

Loving care

r-i p-p-l-i-n-g,

restoring faith,

t r a m p l i n g pain,

returning

HOPE.

Help?
Let Me Count the Ways!

Loving, you brought comfort,

Overcoming, you conquered chaos,

Visiting, you said, "I care."

Embracing, you shared grief.

Helping, you revived strength.

Encouraging, you imparted belief.

Listening, you released pain.

Praying, you restored faith.

ORDER FORM

☎ **Telephone Orders:** 1-800-445-6754 (book orders only). Have MasterCard, VISA, AMEX, or Discover ready. **FAX Orders: 512-656-2129.**

Postal Orders: ABBA Publishing. P. O. Box 47910ʙᴋ, San Antonio, TX 78265-7910

Send the following book(s). I may return book(s) for full refund for any reasons, no questions asked. *Borrowed Joy* has 144 pages (4 individual sections and a picture section.) Four booklets of individual sections are available in quantity for group therapy. Call Leslie at (512) 656-3269.

☐ Soft Cover @ $9.95 ☐ Hard Cover @ $14.95

☐ Send info on other writing by author.

Company Name _____

Address _____

City _____

State _____ **Zip** _____

Sales Tax: Please add 8.25% for books shipped to Texas Addresses or send Tax Number.

Shipping $2.25 for first book and $.75 each additional book. (Surface Shipping may take 3 to 4 weeks) (2nd day Air $4.00 each book)

Payment: ☐ Check ☐ Credit Card
☐ VISA ☐ MasterCard ☐ AMEX ☐ Discover

Card Number _____

Name on Card _____

Expiration Date _____

CALL TOLL FREE - ORDER NOW
1-800-445-6754